C000148059

DEALING
WITH
SATANIC
EXCHANGE

Dr. D. K. Olukoya

DEALING WITH SATANIC EXCHANGE

© 2005 DR. D.K. OLUKOYA
ISBN: 978-38233-9-6
1st Published - June 2005 AD
Re-printed - 2011 AD

Publish by:
The Battle Cry Christian Ministries
322, Herbert Macaulay Way,
Yaba P O Box 12272, Ikeja, Lagos
Website: www.battlecrynig com
email: sales@battlecryng.com
Phone 2348033044239,01-8044415

I salute my wonderful wife, Pastor Shade, for her invaluable support in the ministry.

I appreciate her unquantifiable support in the book ministry as the cover designer, art editor and art adviser

All Scripture quotation is from the King James Version of the Bible

TABLE OF CONTENTS

CHAPTER ONE

DEALING WITH SATANIC EXCHANGE

A strange occurrence took place in Genesis 48. This incident throws light on a lot of happenings today.

Genesis 48:13 -20: And Joseph took them both, Ephraim in his right hand toward Israel's left hand, and Manasseh in his left hand toward Israel's right hand, and brought them near unto him. And Israel stretched out his right hand, and laid it upon Ephraim's head, who was the younger, and his left hand upon Manasseh's head, guiding his hands wittingly; for Manasseh was the firstborn, And he blessed Joseph, and said, God, before whom my fathers Abraham and Isaac did walk, the God which fed me all my life long unto this day, The Angel which redeemed me from all evil, bless the lads; and let my name be named on them, and the name of my fathers Abraham and Isaac; and let them grow into a multitude in the midst of the earth. And when Joseph saw that his father laid his right hand upon the head of Ephraim, it displeased him: and he held up his father's hand, to remove it from Ephraim's head unto Manasseh's head. And Joseph said unto his father, Not so, my father- for this is the firstborn; put thy right hand upon his head. And his father refused, and said, I know it, my son, I know it: he also shall become a people, and he also shall be great: but truly his younger brother shall be greater than he, and his seed shall become a multitude of nations. And he blessed them that day, saying, In thee shall Israel be bless, saying, God make thee as Ephraim and as Manasseh: and he set Ephraim before Manasseh.

Joseph wanted his father, Jacob to pray for his children. One was older and the other younger. The elder one was supposed to be positioned at the right hand of the father. The younger was to be positioned on the left hand because of his position in the family.

VIRTUE TRANSFERRED AND EXCHANGED

Joseph took the children to Jacob with the senior on the right and the junior on the left. This was done so that Jacob might lay his right hand upon the senior and the left hand on the junior. But let us take note of what Jacob did in verse 14.

Genesis 48:14: And Israel stretched out his right hand, and laid it upon Ephraim's head, who was the younger, and his left hand upon Manasseh's head, guiding his hands wittingly; for Manasseh was the first born.

Jacob crossed his hands, so that the hand that was supposed to be on the senior would go to the junior and the hand that was supposed to be laid on the junior would be upon the senior There was an exchange. That was how the virtues of Manasseh who was the firstborn were transferred and he could no longer find his feet.

Take up this prayer point: "Every spiritual exchange of my virtues die in the name of Jesus"

According to the scriptures, Joseph complained and protested the arrangement. He told the father that Manasseh was the eldest and Ephraim the youngest. Joseph then removed his father's right hand and attempted putting it on Manasseh's head. His father refused saying that he knew the eldest and the youngest. That was how the blessings of Manasseh were transferred.

EVIL TRANSFERRED AND EXCHANGED

The meaning of this is that it is possible to take someone else's virtues and transfer it. It is possible for an exchange to take place. Let us take a look at 2 kings 5:27

2 Kings 5:27: The leprosy therefore of Naaman shall cleave unto thee, and unto thy seed for ever. And he went out from his presence a leper as white as snow.

This was a pronouncement from prophet Elisha. The lesson here is that sickness can be transferred. The leprosy of Naaman was exchanged. The leprosy got transferred to Gehazi while the good health of Gehazi got transferred to Naaman .

Eccl 8:14 There is a vanity which is done upon the earth; that there be just men, unto whom it happeneth according to the work of the wicked; again, there be wicked men, to whom it happeneth according to the work of the righteous: I said that this also is vanity.

This verse could be translated thus: There is a common happening, on earth. There are righteous men whose righteousness is exchanged for the punishment of the wicked. There are wicked men too whose wickedness is exchanged with the benefits of the righteous.

This means that an exchange can take place. The Bible says;

Daniel 4:16: Let his heart be changed from man's, and let a beast's heart be given unto him; and let seven times pass over him.

This means that a person' heart can be exchanged. The organs of a person's body can be changed. There can be an evil exchange.

We have heard and seen cases of victims, who by beating their domestic servants, the stripes of the beating were appearing on the person who was doing the beating. There was an exchange.

Jesus said something amazingly outstanding in the book of Luke.

Luke 10:5-6: And into whatsoever house ye enter, first say, Peace be to this house. And if the son of peace be there, your peace shall rest upon it: if not, it shall turn to you again.

Here peace is an entity. It can move forward and

backward. It can be given, and it can be withdrawn.

All the things needed to make your life meaningful exist as entities in the spiritual world. They could be stolen; they could be transferred and exchanged.

SATANIC EXCHANGE EXAMINED

To exchange means to take out something completely and replace it with another. This is a strategy which the enemy has continued to use successfully. There is evil exchange or satanic transfer. It is possible for the virtues to be stolen and replaced.

Pray thus; "Anything stolen from my life as a baby arise and locate me in the name of Jesus"

PROSPERITY TRANSFER

Many years ago, a man who was looking for a way of making money went to a fetish doctor. The man was given certain options. He was asked to bring the head of his mother. If he does so, he would be very rich but would live beyond fifty years. He rejected the option. He was told that another option was to go and sleep in a graveyard on the top of the grave of a rich man for 201 days. Within the 201 days, he would not go to the bathroom. He was told that if he complied, he would be extremely rich but after he had gotten the money, strangers would bury him. The man rejected the second option. He was given another option. A big lizard was shown unto him. He was told to swallow it alive. He was instructed that anytime he needed money, he should vomit the lizard and the lizard would vomit money. But, he was told that he would only have money for three years. But if he coughed and the lizard refused to vomit money, his stomach would get swollen and he would die. He refused that option also. He demanded for another option. In answer to his demand he was asked to feed on blood for three months without eating anything. He would have to drink only blood.

He too must supply blood at three days interval. If he failed to carry out the instruction, he would die. Again, he rejected the option.

He was later given another option. The option was to look for three rich women and bring materials from their bodies. It could be their fingernails or hairs. This was needed so that their virtues could be transferred to him. He accepted the last option. This true story shows how the enemy cleverly transfers people's prosperity and virtues.

Some men have slept with the kind of women they should not sleep with. There are some women too, who have slept with the kind of men they should not have slept with. Through this their virtues and prosperity were taken away.

It is possible to pray and recover your transferred virtues.

Once you have repented and you are born again you have the right to demand that your virtues should be restored.

GREAT DELIVERANCE

There was a girl who was the best in the mathematics class. She woke up on a particular day and became insane, suddenly. The father ran to the Church and requested that prayer should be offered for his daughter. Just as the man of God was about to pray, the spirit of God told him, "Son do not border to pray. Tell the man to go to his father (The grandfather of the girl) and ask that a small coffin buried at the centre of his living room be exhumed. Open the coffin and the girl shall be made whole" The father of the girl kept pleading for prayer but the man of God insisted that the divine instruction should be carried out.

Eventually, the man went to his father and demanded the coffin at the centre of the parlour be brought out in obedience to the instruction given by the man of God.

The grandfather asked the man to describe the man of God who asked him to carry out such strange instruction. After the description, the grandfather said, "You can carry on the instruction" The coffin was brought out. Inside the small coffin were some fetish materials and a white paper with the name of the girl written on it. The things were destroyed. That was how the girl recovered from insanity, and she became normal again. The old man did not want to die so he kept using another life to exchange for his life.

MAJOR EXAMPLES

The devil has no power to create anything. But he is the most successful robber in the universe. It is one thing for the enemy to steal a man's wedding certificate; it is another thing for him to steal the husband or the wife. A small thief may steal your document but a clever thief will steal your intelligence. Since the devil is a clever thief he can steal, transfer and exchange your virtue. There are some major exchanges that the enemy carries out.

1. **There Is Spirit Exchange:** A terrible spirit may enter into a person and take over the person's personality. There will be constant misfortune. It is possible for someone to be alive while the real essence of the person is gone. The human essence has been withdrawn, of course,

blessings will not come the way of such person.

2.   **Body Exchange:** There are people who look older than their age. Once some people enter into a place their presence invites irritation. That is why we often hear testimonies concerning the fact that during prayer a whole personality went out of somebody's body.

3.   **Brain Exchange:** The enemy knows that without your brain, you cannot succeed in your academics. There are many cases in which witches were compelled to remove the intelligence of brilliant people and replace it with the brain of a goat or a cow.

4.   **Child Exchange:** A pregnant woman was attacked, and her baby was taken out of the womb and replaced with an evil foetus through satanic surgery.

5.   **Wealth Exchange:** This occurs when the money a person ought to make is transferred and exchanged with counterfeit money. The hairs of the individuals are often taken away in order to manipulate their wealth.

6.   **Virtues Exchange:** The virtues of a person is transferred, and exchanged. The owner of the

virtues will continue to experience dis-favour while the individual who receives the exchanged virtue will continue to enjoy favour.

7. **Talent Exchange:** This happens when the talent of a person is stolen or transferred to another person.

8. **Partner Exchange:** This is when the husband or the wife which the person ought to marry had been taken away.

9. **Promotion Exchange:** The promotion due to some people are exchanged and given to those who do not merit it.

10. **Age Exchange:** Those who are old can decided to grow younger through satanic manipulation.

11. **Health Exchange:** Good health can be exchanged.

12. **Organ Exchange:** Organs can also be exchanged.

SYMPTOMS OF SATANIC EXCHANGE

How do you know if you are suffering from satan exchange? These are the signs.

1. First born demotion
2. Serious failure at the edge of serious breakthroughs.
3. Unexplainable health failure.
4. Brain failure.
5. Memory loss
6. Having children who become your enemy.
7. If you are a girlish boy or boyish girl.
8. Wrong marriage
9. Stagnancy.
10. Dis-favour
11. Vagabond life
12. Insanity
13. Sad countenance
14. Contrast personality
15. Making unexplainable and unpardonable errors.
16. Blackout
17. Horrible nightmares: Horrible dreams hinder or prevent good things.
18. Desiring good things but unable to carry it out.
19. Getting married in the dream
20. Cycle of poverty
21. Having constant failure and disappointment.
22. Life of trouble and hardship
23. Seeing dead or mad people in the dream.

I want you to know that the devil cannot create but he can transfer. When the devil realizes that his children are in need of anything, he will locate those who have what the children of the devil want. He will steal those things and transfer it to his children It is because the devil cannot create anything for his children.

THE WAY OUT OF SATANIC EXCHANGE

1. Repent, give your life to Jesus and be born again.

2. Pull down the altar of satanic Exchange.

3. Command a reverse

PRAYER POINTS

1 I reject the exchange of my virtues in Jesus name.

2. Withdraw my stolen virtues in Jesus name

CHAPTER TWO

THE RAGE OF THE EVIL HORN

Take these prayer points with holy anger as a prelude to this powerful message.

1   "Every hunter looking for my star, die in the name of Jesus"

2.   "Every witchcraft bird flying for my sake I bury you now in the name of Jesus".

3.   "Every arrow fired against my breakthroughs die in the name of Jesus".

4.   "Serpent in my family house die, in the name of Jesus".

5.   "Every power that has prepared a pit for me shall fall into it in the name of Jesus".

6.   My life must move on by fire in the name of Jesus".

My prayer for you as you go through this chapter is that the power that caused you to be stagnant shall be disgraced.

This prophetic message shall be anchored on the book of Zechariah 1:18

Zechariah 1:18: Then lifted I up mine eyes, and saw, and behold four horns.

The evil horns are scattering horns. They are the horns of demotion. But thank God for the ministry of the carpenters that come to threaten them.

WHAT ARE HORNS?
Horns are natural weapons found on the head of animals.

Horns are used in the Bible as containers for the anointing oil. In the Bible horns are also used as musical instrument. Horns were placed at the four corners of the altars in the Bible.

There is a record in the Bible about the horns of the wicked. This can be found in the book of Psalms.

Psalm 75:10: All the horns of the wicked also will cut off; but the horns of the righteous shall be exalted.

THE EVIL HORN

Every year has its own characteristic pattern. Every year has its own signs. It has its own special features.

Each time you begin a new year, the year enters into a fast track. The year is always in a hurry to close up. Time does not wait for anyone. It is advisable for you to quicken your pace in order to catch up with fast moving time. A new season brings a kind of transition and exchange depending on your disposition to the past.

Life can be exchanged for life. Those who serve God and those who refuse to serve Him must be distinguish one from another as the year passes by. If the saints of God can be serious, much more exploits can be accomplish in the course of time because God has given us time in order to make outstanding accomplishments and bring about definite changes in our lives.

There is a height you can attain in God where defeat wit become a thing of the past. It is my prayer that the Lord will take you there in the name of Jesus.

Your stolen destiny shall be recovered in the name of Jesus, The long drawn battle which you have been fighting before shall come to an end in Jesus name. The hold of the wicked over you shall be broken in Jesus name.

Just as God has special packages for His children everywhere, so also has the devil programmed evil package for a good number of people. Nothing should be taken for granted.

A lot of believers who have lost their axe head must look for the axe head in order to progress. Deep spiritual understanding is necessary because we live in the era of the evil horns. Our country (Nigeria) is controlled by four wicked horns. Four different animals represent these horns. The first animal is the crocodile, the second, the lion and the third python while the fourth is the shark. Each section of the country is manned by each horn.

There is one horn for the North another one for the South, another for the East and there is one for the West.

These evil horns are very mean, resolute, wicked calculated and wise. They specialize in shedding blood and destroying lives.

They are taskmasters. They know how to use men to manipulate the nation. They scatter and demote. The Bible says that the horns have scattered Judah so that none can lift his head.

As you continue reading this book spare a moment, raise your right hand to the Lord now and shout this prayer, "Any power that does to want me to lift my head, what are you waiting for? Die in the name of Jesus".

The evil horns are heartless. They develop masterpiece designs. They have an unusual understanding of men. These horns are very corrupt.

There is nothing outside their sphere of influence. They are patient and subtle. They leave destruction behind and where they go through. They are bolt fiery and daring. They threaten to kill and actually do so.

Although these horns are spiritual, they have physical, representations. They are the ones tossing people around like furious cows fighting with horns. They are often in terrible rage. The opposition against these horns may be futile if care is not taken.

These horns exercise dominion through violent power. Their delight is to smash, to ruin, to twist, to militate, to distort to disfigure, to darken and to strike anywhere they can be seen. They often use the truth to propagate lies. These are! the reasons believers cannot afford to live carelessly.

These wicked spirits are wicked to the core. It is unfortunate that most time we ignore them. We often overlook them. So called prayer warriors are not bothered about them. That is why they allow them to operate freely and unmolested They are very stubborn and very malignant. They have infiltrated all families and communities.

Oftentimes, these horns try to counterfeit the work of the Holy Spirit. They cooperate with ancestral spirits to deal with people. They produce all kinds of negative and terrible vision. These are terrible sprits indeed and they have fifteen-fold agenda.

AGENDA OF THE EVIL HORNS

1. **Management:** They want to manage people's lives.

2. **Temptation:** They make people to face all kinds of temptations.

3. **Obsession:** They allow people to move about freely whereas a particular area of life is in bondage. That is why people come to the house of God, get involved in spiritual activities and yet the same people get busy with masturbation each night.

4. **Oppression:** Evil horns oppress.

5. **Harassment:** They harass their victims.

6. **Possession:** They seek to possess people so that they are spiritually strangulated.

7. **Antagonism:** They antagonize those who are bent to move ahead in life.

8. **Intimidation:** They love to intimidate people.

9. **Dominate:** They seek to exercise full control over people.

10. **Seduction:** the evil horns cause men and women to fall flat and suffer sexual harassment.

11. **Initiate:** They initiate people into different occult and evil groups.

12. **Marital Turbulence:** They cause trouble in many homes.

13. **Manipulation:** They are there to manipulate people at will

14. **Evil Magnet:** They magnetise evil to lives in families

15. **Evil Companions:** They programme unfriendly friend who cause problems into the lives of people.

16. **SYMPTOMS OF THE ATTACK OF THE POWER OF HORNS.**

1. Seeing dead relatives in the dream: If you experience this, you must pray against satanic horns.

2. If your notice that when you are at a particular location you have certain dreams but by the time you leave for another location that kind of dream vanishes and another kind of dream begins Then,

you need to pray against the power of the horns.

3. If you have seen ghosts physically, you are already under the control of evil horns.

4. Do you notice chains of bad luck? It means you are already under their control.

5. Have you discovered that anywhere you go, your presence ignites hatred? It means you are already under their control.

6. Do you experience barriers? Is there anything keeping you from moving forward? Has a particular thing become a stumbling block.? Then you need to pray against the ministry and the activities of the evil horns.

7. Do you notice that you go to the wrong Churches? If you remain in a fake Church you are troubled by the power of evil.

8. Do you have terrible fear and constant failure in life? Then you are engulfed by powers of the evil horn.

9. Do you manifest suicidal tendencies? It means you are already under their control.

10. Do you notice disfavour anywhere you go? It

means you are under their control.

11. Do you desire to always do the right thing but unable to carry the right thing out? It means you are already under their control.

12. Perhaps before you get to a place, somebody might have gotten there and received your benefit. This means that the activities of the horns are at work in your live. Do you suffer extreme restlessness? Do you have severe health problems? If yes, you need to pray against the powers of the evil horns.

13. Do you always get attracted to an evil personality? If yes then you are under the manipulation of the evil horns'

These spirits cause disaster. Therefore, you need to pray your way out of disaster. Each life and family must determine to pray in order to cancel any form of disaster. The lack of deliverance of individuals results in lack of collective deliverance.

The restlessness of individuals when combined together becomes general restlessness. Individual fears when summed together become general fear. Today, you must make up your mind that, you will arise, shine and arrest that the power of horns that scatter. Pray that such power will not function in your life and destiny. These horns have already overpowered and killed multitudes. They operate with aggression and anger. The Bible says;

Psalm 2:1- 4: Why do the heathen rage, and the people imagine a vain thing? The kings of the earth set themselves, and the rulers take counsel together, against the LORD, and against his anointed, saying, Let us break their bands asunder, and cast away their cords from us. He that sitteth in the heavens shall laugh: the Lord shall have them in derision.

There are levels of demons. There are some fearful demons -that anyone could easily cast them out. But, according to Psalm 2, there are some spirits that have the audacity to gather themselves against the Lord and against His anointed. This kind of spirits cannot be easily driven out.

SPIRITUAL CARPENTERS

We thank God for the rod of iron. We thank God for the Carpenters that can cut off the evil horns. These spiritual carpenters can be made to work on your behalf. Ask them to pray and cut off every evil horn working against your destiny. Raise your hand into the heavenlies and pray; "Oh carpenter of God, break the horns of darkness in the name of Jesus"

THOSE WHO MUST BREAK LOOSE FROM EVIL HORNS

1. Those who have been sentenced to profitless, hard work.

2. Those who are expecting marital break-throughs.

3. Those who want to conquer failure at the edge of success.

4. Those who are seeking for profitable employment.

5. Those who are constantly harassed by witchcraft powers.

6. Those who are harassed by the spirit of death.

7. Those who are failing in their assignment or calling.

8. Those who are experiencing unexplainable business failure.

9. Those whose promotions have been stolen by the power of the horns.

10. Those who are under collective bondage or captivity.

CHAPTER THREE

THE DESTRUCTIVE DREAMS

The enemy has carefully chosen the hour of sleep to perpetrate havoc against the lives and destinies of people. This fact is made very clear below:

Matt 13:25: But while men slept, his enemy came and sowed tares among the wheat, and went his way.

But why has the enemy targetted the hour of sleep? The hour of sleep is the time when men are not alert. That is why a lot of satanic activities take place at that hour.

Many of the things which man grapples with as a result of the plantations of the devil are evil works which man realises long after the evil farmer had gone his way. From this reference it is clear that the enemy did not wait to water what he has planted. The devil must have reached the potentialities of his wicked seeds.

He knows that immediately the heart of man is suitable and nutritious enough, the seed will automatically grow.

IGNORANCE KILLS

The Almighty God uses dreams to benefit His children. This can be confirmed in the book of Job 33:13-18.

Job 33:13-18: Why dost thou strive against him? for he giveth not account of any of his matters. For God speaketh once, yea twice, yet man perceiveth it not In a dream, in a vision of the night, when deep sleep falleth upon men, in slumbering upon the bed; Then he openeth the ears of men, and sealeth their instruction, That he may withdraw man from his purpose, and hide pride from man. He keepeth back his soul from the pit, and his life from perishing by the sword.

Although ears could be opened for divine instruction God through dreams could warn man against taking certain decisions. This is done to keep man from the snares of the devil.

A brother had a dream that someone was injecting him on his legs. When he woke up, he felt a slight pain on his legs. He ignored the pain. He did not take any action. Two weeks later, he had become very ill. By the time a test was carried out, it was reported that he had HIV. A little knowledge would have enabled the brother to sort out the problem.

SOME BASIC AND FUNDAMENTAL STATEMENTS

Let us consider some nuggets

1. The realm of the dream is as important as the physical realm.

2. Dreams are means of communication.

3. You are a product of your dreams.

4. It is very dangerous to ignore what goes on in the dream because dreams monitor what is going on in the spirit world.

5. Your dream never lies although you may not understand what it is saying.

6. Your dream can reveal your past as well as your future.

7. Your dream can expose the enemies that are gathered against you.

8. All dreams have unique messages although may not be understood. The dream may look disorganized and disjointed yet there is a message in it.

9. Satan is much more interested in influencing our dreams. Satan attacks people with sickness and all kinds of failure through the dream. The devil has manipulated dreams and introduced automatic failure to their lives. The devil has transformed himself to an angel of light to deceive people in their dreams.

10. God also can use dreams as a way of preventing His people from danger. God can also use dreams to expose, to His people, enemy's plans against them.

11. The enemy knows that once he can influence your dream life then he can influence so many things.

Many years ago, I spent time praying for a sister When she got home after the first day of the prayer, she had a dream. In her dream she saw herself before a mighty king who sat on a giant throne. The king then asked the sister, "Who asked you to go for prayer and who asked you to consult that man for prayers? If you go there again, I will bury your glory" The king further said, "Don't you know that you are a queen?' That was the first time she had such a dream. The king said "To prove to you that you belong to this place we are going to wipe off your dream memory". From that day she could no longer remember what she dreamt about.

The enemy was able to deal with her. If not for God'! intervention. She would have been captured by the enemy.

12. The evil seeds which the enemy plants in the dream may take so many years before they germinate. If it is not arrested on time, the fault is yours.

13. There are many classes of dreams.

Class One - This category of people do not dream at all, This class of people needs to pray deliverance and overhauling prayers. The problem is that this class of people see nothing in the dream concerning what the enemy is planning against them. If this class of people do not dream they will not have any idea concerning the enemy's plan to deal with them, they will be ignorant if God is also ready to bless them. They will not know anything.

Class Two - These are eraser dreamers. When this class of people wake up they will forget their dreams. They will only realise that they had a dream which had been forgotten.

Class Three - This group of dreamers suffer chronic inability to recall their dreams.

Class Four - These are people with meaningless dreams.

Class Five - The vagabond dreamers. These are the kind of dreamers who roam all over the place in their dreams.

Class Six - These are occult dreamers. These dreamers always meet people whom they do not know in their. dreams.

Class Seven - These are dream dreamers. The depth of the dreams go beyond the surface.

Class eight - These are people who come in contact with trouble through dreams. They dream about trouble each time they dream.

Class Nine - These are reverse dreamer. If they drear that someone gives then money, it means somebody will steal their money. Anything they see in the dream will turn out to be negative.

Class Ten - These are people who go through nightmare.

Class Eleven - The prophetic dreamers. Whenever this: class of dreamers dream it is highly prophetic

There is. nothing the enemy can not do in the dream. He paralyze, steal or turn a person's life upside down

The enemy can place his hand on the body and remove anything he likes. The enemy can introduce any evil substance to the body. Through dreams the enemy has caged multitudes. If the victim remains ignorant the suffering will continue. You must address negative dreams today.

PRAYER POINTS

I want you to address certain problems in your prayer:

1. Thou that troubleth my Israel my God shall trouble you today in the name of Jesus.

2. Holy Ghost fire arise, destroy every resistance to the shinning of my star in the name of Jesus.

3. "Every seed of darkness planted into my life in the dream die in the name of Jesus"

4. "Every satanic dream that is afflicting my future die in the name of Jesus"

5. "Every power hunting my star in the dream what are you waiting for? Die in the name of Jesus".

6. Every arrow of death fired against me in my dream, backfire in the name of Jesus.

7. "Every dream sponsored by witchcraft powers die in the name of Jesus"

8. "Every strongman dedicated to my dream, hear the word of the Lord appear now and be paralysed in the name of Jesus"

9. "Oh ground hear the word of the Lord open and swallow the strongman that is dedicated to my dream in the name of Jesus"

CHAPTER FOUR
I SHALL LAUGH LAST

Life is full of vicissitudes. There are certain situations and problems that have defiled every solution. All efforts to stem evil tides have ended in futility. Man's desperate search for joy and 'happiness has not yielded the desired results. The storms of life have taken a heavy toll on the lives of many. The rage of the waters has kept many heads submerged and buried. You should not be ignorant of the fact that many academic geniuses have been reduced to wrecks as a result of the manipulations of the enemy. In fact, the situation is rather becoming more complex by the day.

I want to proclaim to all and sundry that God's power knows no limitations. Impossibility is not found in God vocabulary In fact, God desires to start his operations at the very moment when men have exhausted every ounce of energy. The Master of the storms can do all things. The only thing he needs to say is "Peace be still" and all raging storms will be calm.

There has never been any undertaking of God that has not seen the light of the day. Never has it been heard that the Almighty God is a failure. He has never and will never fail. Your predicaments can not be above the power of God. It is possible for you to have tried different alternatives to get your problems solved and none has yielded the desired result. I want to tell you that you can bounce back into the joy of God. The power of God can remove every strange hand from your life. You can be totally emancipated from the shackles of the enemy.

You will laugh last. The power of God can change the status quo and give you a new song and name. I want to prophetically declare unto you that the power of God will collide; with your problems. An end has come to all the manipulation of the devil and the host of darkness concerning your life Jesus must reign in your life! God's name must be glorified and shame be given to the enemies. Nothing whatsoever can stand against your breakthrough because the time has come for God to put laughter in your mouth. Call upon God in this prayer point:

1.   My hands shall bring forth signs and wonders to the glory of God and to the shame of Satan.

Satan and his cohorts are the ones behind mysterious occurrences. That is why you need to arm yourself with the necessary spiritual warfare tools if you don't want to fall a casualty. The daily destruction of lives should give us concern Even if you have been entrenched in spiritual famine, the mighty hand of God can bring you back and relocate you for blessings. At the end laughter and testimonies will fill your mouth.

Job 5:22: At destruction and famine thou shall laugh: neither shall thou be afraid of the beasts of the earth.

Your God will manifest. Maybe, unbelievers are challenging you to show where your God is. Don't worry. Don't panic. The God of hosts whose abode is in heaven and who rules and dominates the world will come to your rescue. I want you to know that delay is not denial. The plans and purposes of God for your life will be materialized whether the devil likes it or not. The boastings of the enemies will be put to shame because it is the will of God for you to prosper and triumph. Victory lies in Christ Jesus.

You can triumph over the wiles of the enemies with God on your side. Only put your trust in the Everlasting Arm and your heart desires will be answered.

A CASE STUDY

At every age and time, God has been in the business of putting laughter in the mouth of His children. No matter the trouble persecution or trials the mighty arms of God will always show up to succour His beloved. Of course, the enemies may boast, brag and even threaten, but God knows the right time to show up to defend His own. My prayer is that the Almighty God will show up to bless your life in the midst of satanic manipulations in Jesus name.

The account below aptly captures an

interesting story of how God fought for His people in spite of the boastings of the enemy.

2 Chro. 32:9: After this did Sennacherib king of Assyria send his servants to Jerusalem, (but he himself laid siege against Lachish, and all his power with him) unto Hezekiah king of Judah, and unto all Judah that were at Jerusalem, saying,

What you have read above is tantamount to what myriads of people across the globe are facing. Many lives and destinies have been terminated as a result of the operation of evil forces that are marauding about and lurking for unstable souls. There are many people who are living a hellish life right on the face of the earth due to the power of darkness. In fact, a great number of people are considering suicide as the best option to their predicaments. This has led to the enlargement of hell. Hell fire is receiving an uncountable number of souls who have been threatened and afflicted by the enemies on earth.

The condition of this set of people could be best describe as moving from frying pan to fire. All these have given me the burden to pour my heart out and white. And, I believe that your life will not be the same as you go through this book in Jesus name.

THERE IS HOPE!

Never give up! You need not to throw in the towel because God has not finished with your life. Tell me, why must satan cut short your life when God still wants to use your life for the divine purpose? Satan is not your creator.

You are wonderfully and marvelously made by God Almighty. Let it be registered in your heart that God cares. He knows your troubles, predicaments and problems. He can save and He can heal if you can follow the divine blueprint.

All the years I have spent in the ministry tells me that there is nothing impossible for God to do. In fact, I cannot express all the testimonies that God had done in a single book. All I want you to do is to bury your unbelief in other to brighten the future. I want you to forget the past threats, turbulence and trials of the devil because the finger of God is ready to open a new leave and rewrite your history on a fresh and new page.

Get ready for divine surprise and encounter. The mighty hand of God has made the barren to be a source of blessings to countless generations. God can bring something out of nothing because He rules in Heaven and on earth. Even if you have been stamped with "person a non grata", power can still change hands to make you the most favoured. It is then all men will call you the favoured of God because you are highly favoured.

Have you been crying all the days long without any help forthcoming? Stop crying! Your cries and tears will make the devil and all his hosts to be happier. Look up to your heavenly father and your creator. An end has come to satan's dominion and activities in your life and family. The idol of your father's house that has been speaking woes to your destiny must be cut asunder. Every yokes and curses that has been barricading and killing your joy must be destroyed by the anointing of the Almighty.

Let it be known that the breath of God is upon the pages you are reading and the fire of God can flow into you right now. Only believe and it will be unto you according to your faith. You can be delivered. If you can follow the principles of deliverance, your deliverance can be achieved today. Also, I don't want to know who has placed the curses upon your head or the type of curses it may be. Whether the curses are national, territorial or family curses, God's hand can reach forth to break those curses. The promise of your deliverance can be found in the verse below:

Isaiah 10:27: And it shall come to pass in that day, that his burden shall be taken away from off thy shoulder, and his yoke from off thy neck, and the yoke shall be destroyed because of the anointing.

WHO IS GOD?

A proper understanding of who God is will help you to be positioned for the mighty hand of God to deliver you from the shackles of the devil. God is the Mighty One. He has all power and exercises all strength. His authority is recognized on the earth in heaven and underneath the earth. God Almighty is the most powerful and the strongest. He divided the Red Sea by His Mighty hand. He even created the universe and all the things in the cosmos.

All the angels were created by God as well. And to crown it all, He is your creator If He is your creator, you need not panic anytime the storms of life arise. What you need to do is to go back to your creator and get things right with Him. And you need to know that God is merciful, kind and caring. He will not in any way cast away those who call upon His name with sincerity and truthfulness.

Now tell me, what is the problem in your life that you think defies solution? Humanly speaking, there are some problems that are not fathomable to the human mind. In fact, there is a limit to which the medical world can go in dealing with human problems. Only God is

DEALING WITH SATANIC EXCHANGE

unlimited. There is no situation, circumstances, problem, predicament that God cannot solve. The hand of God has done it before and yours will not be an exception because you are His creature.

THE DIVINE DECLARATION

I have told you that human extremities are God's opportunities for proving His extra ordinary feats, The word of God for this generation and for all generations can be found in the Bible. The Almighty God has come out to give a divine declaration to show that there is nothing difficult for him to do.

Human beings are prone to doubt the power of God but the divine declaration should re-echo in your ears 'till you will leave the face of the Earth. Let me show you the divine declaration so that you can believe the incredible and thereby achieve extra ordinary feats.

Jer. 32:27: Behold, I am the LORD, the God of all flesh: is there anything too hard for me?

What did you read in the verse above? God Almighty; the creator of heaven and earth is asking a question and also giving a resounding declaration. The King of kings and the Lord of lords wants you to know that your problem is not beyond redemption. As long as God lives (and of course He will live throughout eternity), no situation in human's life is impossible for God. Let this divine declaration be your daily meditations when you are faced with a dilemma. Proclaim it to the devil and the enemies that your redeemer lives. And that there is nothing too hard for him to do.

DELAY IS NOT DENIAL

In God's time table, delay is never a denial. In fact, the delay you have may be there to prove the power of God. The common denominator among all those that had one form of delay is that they receive distinct blessings from the Lord. This should tell you that God can decide to do as He wishes, His rulings are final and not open for redress in the court of heaven.

Abraham had a delay in child bearing for decades but he never gave up his faith in God. His feet were unmoved, and his faith did not waver. God put surprises in his mouth and he got Isaac; the promised child. Isaac and Rebecca also had delays in child birth and by the time God visited them, they had two great twins.

Hannah also had delay in child birth. She was vexed and provoked beyond measure. This provocation made her to settle her problem of barrenness once and for all at Shiloh. She was undaunted, determined and resolute. And, at the end of the day she had a divine visitation that turned her life around. Not only was she given a child, she was able to give birth to Samuel; one of the greatest prophet of Israel. The life of Lazarus whom Jesus raised back to life further tells us that delay is not denial. Before Lazarus died, he had been indisposed for some time and Mary and Martha had gone to inform Jesus so that he could heal his sickness. But it all happened suddenly that Lazarus died before the arrival of the Great Healer. At this point, the situation of things could be best described as hopeless.

However, Jesus came to the scene to show that he has Power over death and the tomb. Therefore, considering your predicament as good as nothing will not help you. Christ Jesus has the power to heal, deliver and even set the captives free. How great is our God? The creator of Heaven and earth stood by the tomb and issued a command.

John 11 :43-44: And when he thus had spoken he cried with a loud voice Lazarus, come forth. And he that was dead came forth, bound hand and foot with grave clothes: and his face was bound about with a napkin. Jesus saith unto them Loose him, and let him go.

Lazarus who had been dead and stinking for four day! heard the voice of Jesus, Death could not hold him but it released him. And, at the end the incredible happened.

When the power of Jehovah collided with your plights, be rest assured that your joy is imminent. It does not really matter the long years you have spent under satanic oppression The Lord can put laughter in your mouth and cause you to have a testimony that will shake the whole world. Whoever may be behind your problem and whatever may be behind your plight must hear the voice of the Almighty because your set time has come.

THE SET TIME

There is what is known as the divine timing in spiritual warfare. At God's set time, your miracle can not be hindered by anybody or anyone. At the set time of God, the Lord visited the family of Abraham and granted him the desired blessing. At God's set time, even unbelief could not hinder the power of God in the family of Elizabeth and Zachariah. The barren womb had to hear the word of God to change the order of things Menopause in the medical parlance was proved wrong by the power and authority of God.

It is impossible by two immutable things for God to lie. Even if it will take God to speak to nature and cosmological entities, the word of God will have to come to pass. Have you forgotten what God did during the time of Elijah and Joshua? Prophet Elijah under the inspiration of the Almighty gave a prophetic declaration which shut the heaven and held up the rain. Of course, the heaven was locked and there was no rain upon the earth, A man kept the key of nature in his hands!

Joshua also called upon the name of God and issued a word of decree to tell the sun to stand still until all the enemies of God would be destroyed and there was a divine attestation to the decree. I have to tell you all these so that you will know that God has a standard which no other power can compromise. Not even all the hosts of hell in the sea, on earth or in heaven can say no when the Almighty God wants to put laughter in your mouth. They may brag but your God is great and mighty.

Have you been suffering from one ailment or the other? Is your health deteriorating and aggravating everyday and moment? Do you have a problem that you can hardly share with people? Are you disturbed in the dream by spirit wife or husband? Whatever mysterious occurrences that might be trailing your life has to hear the word of God because enough is enough. Maybe, your enemies have been deriding and laughing you to scorn, don't worry because there is hope. The message that God has for you can be found in the verses below:

Ps 30:5-6: For his anger endureth but a moment; in his favour is life: weeping may endure for a night, but joy cometh in the morning. And in my prosperity I said I shall never be moved.

I want you to take this prayer point with holy aggression:

Every power challenging my God, be disgraced in the name of Jesus.

CHAPTER FIVE

LAUGHTER SPIRITUAL WEAPON

L aughter may seem to be a strange warfare strategy but it works. In the Bible, laughter could mean to mock, to deride or to scorn. When you can laugh in spite of whatever revival satan is holding against your life, the enemy is put to fight very quickly.

Many years back, a sister got an accommodation somewhere in the city. When she entered the room and parlour, the landlady cautioned the sister against entering the last room vehemently. She made it known to the sister that no one enters the last room and even made her to sign a document in respect of this warning. As the sister entered her accommodation, she discovered that the room was always under lock at all times.

The sister became curious and inquisitive about the mystery behind the room that was always under lock. But one day, the landlady forgot to lock the room and the sister- took a bold step to enter the room. The sister entered and was shocked beyond description at the horrible thing She saw inside To her amazement, she found a human being sitting on a chair, looking dazed and dead.

There was a calabash of money on the head of the lifeless human being and money was found in the room. To compound the problem the sister decided to confront the landlady without having the necessary power to do so. This decision culminated into the problems of her life. At the time the landlady heard that the cat had been let out of the bag she gave the sister a quick notice but the sister was adamant. She complained of having not being able to finish spending the time she paid for. Her obstinate gesture made her to have marital problem. Almost about seven proposed marriages could not see the light of the day because of the wicked operations of the landlady.

The sister usually had a horrible encounter with a monkey few days to her planned marriage. In the dream, the monkey would enter her room through the window and fight with the sister, The following day, the suitor would suddenly walk up to her to cancel the planned marriage.

On one fateful day, she decided to take the bull by the horns and prayed the prayer of the death of her Hamman. She prayed through until she received heavenly assurance. While the sister was planning another marriage, she had a regular and usual visit by the monkey in the dream. Since she had prevailed in the spiritual realm, what she did to the monkey was to issue a command. She only said; "You monkey, stand at attention in the name of Jesus"! The monkey had no option than to stand. She asked the monkey to tell her the person that sent it and the monkey replied that the landlady had sent it. The sister then told the monkey to go back to where it came from and that was the end of the long standing battle. The following morning the landlady was gone

Do you know that God can laugh through you? I believe you know that God is sometimes called the God of Abraham He gave Abraham a child of promise after long years of barrenness. And what do you think is the meaning of Isaac the promised child? Isaac means laughter. In other words God laughed at human's knowledge to do what human being: would consider impossible. God can likewise laugh through you at this time in Jesus name. The passage below further buttresses the fact that God also laughs:

Ps 2:1-4: Why do the heathen rage, and the people imagine a vain thing? The kings of the earth set themselves, and the rulers take counsel together, against the LORD, and against his anointed, saying, Let us break their bands asunder, and cast away their cords from us. He that sitteth in the heavens shall laugh: the Lord shall have them in derision.

Who did God laugh at? God laughed at his enemies who are also in a way the enemies of the children of God. People who oppose the gospel and the people of God are standing as the enemies of God. Saul of Tarsus was an arch enemy of God. He went about to imprison the Christians he was able to lay hands on. But, God met him on his way to Damascus and laughed at him. He was touched by God. and instantly commissioned to proclaim the gospel throughout the length and breadth of the earth.

And, at the end of the day, he became a mighty instrument in the hands of the Almighty through which the gospel got to the Gentile nations and to us by extension.

All those who hate the truth are the enemies of God and the people who are friends of the world. You automatically become the enemy of God once you allow worldliness in your life. The world and God are two parallel lines that cannot meet. It is either you are a friend of the world and automatically qualify as the enemy of God or you are a friend of God and hates the world and all forms of worldliness.

James 4:4: Ye adulterers and adulteresses, know ye not that the friendship of the world is enmity with God? whosoever therefore will be a friend of the world is the enemy of God.

It is a pity if God can laugh at our enemies while we are afraid of them. The enemies may strategize to pull the children of God down but if God is with us our victory is guaranteed. And we are bound to laugh last no matter the wiles of the devil and his cohorts.

Ps 37:12-13: The wicked plotteth against the just, and gnasheth upon him with his teeth. The Lord shall laugh at him: for he seeth that his day is coming.

CHANGE YOUR PRAYER!

A sister discovered that she was having serious problems and she prayed about it but nothing was forthcoming. She had a revelation one night. An angel came and told her to change her prayers. The angel further told her to change her prayers to: "I refuse to be donated to the enemy"! She questioned the angel and was told that she had already been donated to the enemy. The sister told the angel that she was born again and the angel made her to realize that she had already been donated before she gave her life to Christ. Whether you believe or not, I want you to take this prayer point:

I refuse to be donated to the enemy in the name of Jesus.

After the sister had taken this warfare prayer point, her grandmother came to her and advised her never to take the kind of prayer point she prayed again, The sister asked her grandmother whether the prayer point disturbed her but, she was told to stop praying such a prayer point. The "stubborn sister" therefore decided to hold a vigil on the same prayer point. She prayed throughout the night on this prayer point and the following morning, the grandmother could not come out of her room. The sister checked her grandmother's room to find out what was happening. She was surprised to find her unable to rise. The sister asked her grandmother what was wrong but she only managed to say: "you will soon kill somebody".

Maybe, you would expect the sister to stop praying. The sister did not stop praying but she intensified her prayers by organizing three days vigil on the prayer point. And it happened that on the seventh day, the grandmother died! By the time the woman was to be buried, people found a calabash under her bed and inside it, the name of the sister was boldly written and a drop of blood was on the name. It was after this incident that the sister was able to experience a breakthrough in her life.

THE ENEMIES OF GOD

A proper study of your Bible will reveal. Some of the forces of hell that usually oppose the will of God in the lives of God's children. These forces are represented by some names of Biblical characters who gave themselves to the use of the devil.

The spirit of Balaam is the spirit hired to curse God's people. At the end of the day, Balaam had to fall by the sword because it is difficult for anyone to curse those whom God had blessed. Any spirit of Balaam working against you must be utterly destroyed at this time in the name of Jesus.

Another wicked agent of darkness is the spirit of Korah, Dathan and Abiram, This represents the planners of evil in the satanic kingdom. What happened to them? The ground opened up and swallowed them. Whatever plan and evil preparation is going on in the realm of darkness against your life must be swallowed up because God wants to put laughter in your mouth.

There is also the spirit of Goliath that represents terrifying, boastful and threatening enemy. Goliath, in the Bible, was defeated only by one stone from the five stones that David got (the five stones represent the name of Jesus). At the end of the day, Goliath was found on the floor dead and his head was cut off. Whatever children of Goliath that might be troubling your life must receive the judgment of God at this point in time in Jesus name.

The spirit of Pharaoh is another wicked spirit in the realm of darkness As Pharaoh and all his hosts were swallowed up in the Red Sea, God will utterly destroy the spirit of Pharaoh that wants to waste your life in the name of Jesus.

We also have the spirit of Saul that pursued David in the Bible. The spirit of Saul is the spirit of royal pursuers. When this spirit discovers that you are destined for glory and the throne, your life will be its target. This spirit will send different fiery darts of the wicked to waste your life but if you can arm yourself with spiritual weapons, you will not fall a victim. As Saul died by the sword, the spirit of Saul will likewise receive the judgment of God concerning your life in Jesus name.

Moreover, there is a spirit known as the spirit of Ahitophel, It is otherwise referred to as the spirit of the unfriendly friend. This is the spirit of enemies who disguises as friends to report your life to the satanic kingdom. With God on your side, you can have the victory in Christ by prevailing in prayers.

The spirit of Uzziah is the spirit that blocks divine vision and revelation It was not until king uzziah died in the scriptures before prophet Isaiah could see divine vision. Whatever powers that are blocking you from seeing divine vision that will affect your destiny must die by fire in the name of Jesus.

The spirit of Absalom represents household enemy or the enemy within. Absalom in the Bible had to hang himself and die thereby. The "spirit" of Daniel represents the enemies that want to cut short the lives of God's children, The enemies of Daniel in the Bible succeeded in throwing Daniel into the den of lions but God's presence was with him. At the end of the day,- the enemies of Daniel and their families were fed to the hungry lions. And Daniel laughed and rejoiced in the Lord at the end.

The Sanbalat and Tobiah spirits stand for the spirits that hinder good things from being built up, These spirits destroy and diminish the lives of people at an early age. Sanbalal and Tobiah were disgraced by God Almighty. Every spirit of Sanbalat and Tobiah in your life be disgraced in the name of Jesus and you shall laugh last!

The spirit of Herod is the power that destroys potentials, This power can go to any length in the realm of darkness to destroyable potentials. At the end, Herod was slapped by an angel from God and was eaten up by worms instantly.

The spirit of Sennacherub is the power of a boastful and besieging spirit that always seeks to terrorize the people of God. At the end he was destroyed by his own household wickedness. The people he trusted so much were used as an instrument for his fatal destruction.

The spirit of Hamman is the power responsible for planning death against the people of God. They are also responsible for planning the death of good things. In all these, the believer who knows the principles of spiritual warfare prayers will definitely have the last laugh.

God wants to thunder and cause an eruption in the Kingdom of darkness. Enough is enough! Your victory must be got by fire. The hosts of hell must vomit your blessings. God's hands must put an end to failure, barrenness and mystery in your life. Derision, damnation and woe must be the lot of the kingdom of hell. Laughter must fill your mouth as you take the following prayer points with seriousness and faith in Christ.

PRAYER POINTS:

1. Every powers sponsoring demotion against me, be disgraced in the name of Jesus.

2. Every powers consulting the sun and the moon against me fall down and die in the name of Jesus.

3. Every spiritual transaction with the dead, I cancel you now in the name of Jesus.

4. Angels of the living God ransack the land of the living and the land of the dead and recover my stolen blessings in the name of Jesus.

5. Every witchcraft bird limiting my progress, receive the arrow of fire in the name of Jesus.

6. Every spirit of the grave, fall down and die in the name of Jesus.

7. Every agent of nakedness and poverty fall down and die in the name of Jesus.

8. Oh Lord plant me by your traffic light in the name of Jesus

9. Every evil tree planted against me, become rotten in the name of Jesus.

10. My Hamman shall die by fire for my God shall answer by fire in the name of Jesus

11. Every owner of evil load, carry your load, it does not belong to me in the name of Jesus.

12. I shall rise above all the unbelievers around me in the name of Jesus,

13. I shall laugh last over my enemies in the name of Jesus

14 Oh God of success who knows no failure, I claim dumbfounding success in the name of Jesus.

15. I refuse to loose in the name of Jesus,

16. Every root of poverty be destroyed by fire in the name of Jesus.

17. Oh Lord, give me a turnaround breakthrough in the name of Jesus.

18. Every curse issued against my destiny, fall down and die in the name of Jesus.

CHAPTER SIX

DEALING WITH EVIL ARRESTERS

There are evil arresters who must be arrested. The mystery of arresting evil arrester is made plain in 2 Kings chapter 6.

2 Kings 6-8-21: Then the king of Syria warred against Israel, and took counsel with his servants, saying, In such and such a place shall be my camp. And the man of God sent unto the king of Israel, saying, Beware that thou pass not such a place; for thither the Syrians are come down. And the king of Israel sent to the place which the man of God told him and warned him of, and saved himself there, not once nor twice. Therefore the heart of the king of Syria was sore troubled for this thing; and he called his servants, and said unto them, Will ye not shew me which of us is for the king of Israel? And one of his servants said, None, my lord, o king: but Elisha, the prophet that is in Israel telleth the king of Israel the words that thou speakest in thy bedchamber. And he said Go and spy where he is, that I may send and fetch him. And it was told him. saying, Behold, he is in Dothan. Therefore sent he thither horses, and chariots and a great host: and they came by night, and compassed the city about. And when the servant of the man of God was risen early, and gone forth behold, an host compassed the city both with horses and chariots. And his servant said unto him, Alas, my master! how shall we do? And he answered Fear not' for they that be witn us are more than they that be with them. And Elisha prayed, and said, LORD, I pray thee, open his eyes, that he may see. And the LORD opened the eyes of the young man; and he saw: and, behold, the mountain was full of horses and chariots of fire round about Elisha, And when they came down to him, Elisha prayed unto the LORD, and said, Smite this people, I pray thee, with blindness. And he smote them with blindness according to the word of Elisha. And Elisha said unto them, This is not the way, neither is this the city: follow me, and I will bring you to the man whom ye seek But he led them to Samaria. And it came to pass, when they were come into Samaria, that Elisha said, LORD, open the eyes of these men, that they may see And the LORD opened their eyes, and they saw; and, behold, they were in the midst of Samaria. And the king of Israel said unto Elisha, when he saw them, My father, shall I smite them? shall I smite them?

Let us pray before we go into the analysis of the above passage. Pray in this manner; Let all the evil arresters receive blindness in the name of Jesus.

From this passage, we discover that the king of Syria had been waging war against Israel. Whenever the king of Syria laid in ambush, Elisah would always reveal the secret scheme and positioning of the army of the king of Syria That was how the efforts of the king was wasted and rendered null and void.

This development worried and troubled the king of Syria. He accused his army of harboring spies. Little did he realize that Elisha the prophet was the personality who revealed the plans of the king But one of his servants said that it was Elisha who did reveal their military strategies.

FEW LESSONS FROM THIS PASSAGE

1.   **Revelation Of The Secrets Of The Enemy:** There is a need for prayer that every plan and activity

of our enemy should be exposed. A sister once prayed: "I arrest and detain every evil arrester. And I command them to reveal their secrets", she took the prayer points for seven nights running. On the seventh night, she saw someone in bandage. The person appeared to him in the vision with fresh intestines in his hand and said, "Well, since you are praying to arrest the arrester, take your intestines back".

The sister said, "Who are you? Reveal your identity". He revealed himself as a uncle. By the next morning the uncle came physically begging and asking for forgiveness.

2. **Satanic Efforts Rendered Fruitless:** There is a need to pray that all the enemies assigned to us should be committed and assigned to useless activities. There is need to decree that satanic efforts over our lives should be wasted. We must constantly affirm the word . of God to make all the plans of the enemy null and void. For example the phrase of the word of God, which says, "No weapon fashioned against you shall prosper" should always be proclaimed and affirmed.

3. **Satanic Plans Frustrated:** This is accordance with the word of God which says that God frustrates the token of the liars and make diviners mad.

There is need to speak frustrations into every evil activities and evil missions targeted against you.

4. **The Detective Activities Of The Holy Spirit:** The detective activities of the Holy Spirit can break the backbones of the evil soldiers that are at large.

5. **The War Zone:** Benhadad in the passage was a chronic idol worshipper. He worshipped an idol called Rimon which is the Syrian god of war. With the supernatural, intelligence of the Holy Spirit, the position of God's enemy, was known and the enemy was dislodged.

6. **It Is A Useless Activity For The Devil Or Men To try To Outsmart God.**

7. **You Can Sometime Know The Caliber Of A Person By The Kind Of Enemies He Has:** If the devil hates you and he is speaking terrible things against you then you should rejoice because you are in the same camp with Elisha. The next thing to do to overpower evil men is to smite them with blindness.

THE SCHOOL OF FEAR

The servant of Elisha was in the school of fear. He was meditating upon the lies of the devil. He failed to realize that those who were with them are more than those who were with their enemies.

Fear is a torment. Fear is a terror. It hinders God's blessing from reaching you. It makes you see what you are not supposed to see and makes you overlook what you are supposed to see.

Gehazi feared and cried to his master. His master prayed that his eyes should be opened. His eyes got opened and he saw the host of God and the chariot of fire surrounding them and he was assured. The only panacea for fear is to have faith. When you sense the power of God either in vision or in your subconscious mind, fear will die and faith will resurrect.

" When you read the word of God and meditate on the awesome power of God fear will vanish. Fear will jump out of your spirit. When you consider the terrifying power of the Almighty then you will be rest assured that you are in the hollow of His hands. That is the reason the scripture says faith comes by hearing God's word. Faith and fear cannot co-exist.

ELYMAS THE SORCERER

The case of Elymas the sorcerer is another relevant case study. This could be found in the Acts of the apostles,

Acts 13:6-12: And when they had gone through the isle unto Paphos, they found a certain sorcerer, a false prophet, a

Jew, whose name was Bar-Jesus: Which was with the deputy of the country, Sergius Paulus, a prudent man; who called for Barnabas and Saul, and desired to hear the word of God. But Elymas the sorcerer (for so is his name by interpretation) withstood them, seeking to turn away the deputy from the faith. Then Saul, (who also is called Paul,) filled with the Holy Ghost, set his eyes on him, And said, 0 full of all subtilty and all mischief, thou child of the devil, thou enemy of all righteousness, wilt thou not cease to pervert the right ways of the Lord? And now, behold, the hand of the Lord is upon thee, and thou shalt be blind, not seeing the sun for a season. And immediately there fell on him a mist and a darkness; and he went about seeking some to lead him by the hand. Then the deputy, when he saw what was done, believed, being astonished: at the doctrine of the Lord.

Please take note of the phrase "The doctrine of the Lord' In this context, is it the doctrine of-the Lord to make people blind? You can derive answers in the passage and in several other places in the Bible.

Paul did not pat the man at the back or try to convert him He identified his enemy and dealt with him in such a way that deputy was confounded and astonished.

Again note the prayer point of Paul- "Thou shall be blind

UNDERSTANDING THE ARRESTERS

Who are the arresters that must be arrested? The arresters are the following;

1. Eaters Of Flesh And Drinkers Of Blood: They drink people's blood and donate blood at witchcraft meetings. We have seen people in possession of pots full of blood. Such people have confessed that they sucked out such blood from human bodies.

There are many people who use human blood to cook food and sell the food to people. My prayer for you is that those who want to drink your blood shall drink their own blood in the name of Jesus.

2. Ancestral Strongman: There used to be a family of nine. The most educated among them had only elementary primary education. The one who managed to attend secondary school did so because he was born again. He proceeded to the university but his result was withheld. He did not understand the genesis of the problem until he prayed and God showed him a family strongman who was behind the problem.

3. Dream Manipulators: These dream manipulators will show your friend to you in the dream as enemies and your enemies to you as friend so as to get you confused.

4. Satanic Wives And Husbands: A lot of men have spirit wives and many women have spirit husbands. A man with spirit wife will not stay with only one woman.

He will Keep going from one woman to another, thereby incurring diseases.

5. Strange Children: Strange children are often planted in many families to destroy the families. That is why the psalmist prayed that God should deliver him from the hands of strange children.

A man woke up 4;00a,m in the morning and sat on his bed. Suddenly he saw his four year old girl growing up to assume the stature of a big girl. The girl was well dressed and about to go out through the door. Those are the kind of girls found in night parties. The man was amazed and confounded. May God deliver us from strange children.

6. Satanic Spies Or Informants: They reveal the secrets of their targets in order to deal with them. Some people went to spy Elisha and later on went to tell the enemies of Elisha where he was hiding.

7. Satanic Equipment: A14 year old boy confessed to his involvement in witchcraft. He told us that he worked in a department in the spirit world called "Affairs of men" There, they have computers. As they keyed people's names of into the computer, people whose names are keyed in were dying.

8. Counterfeit angels

9. **Evil diviners**

10. **Fake ministers (Physical and spiritual)**

11. **Evil advisers and counselors**

12. **Distributor of infirmities**

13. **Distributors of poverty**

14. **Problem expanders**

15. **Occult Enemies:** There are people who belong to occult societies either reformed or not.
They may be crude or refined. Occult societies are evil arresters.

16. **Satanic Caterers:** These are cooks in the realm of the dream. They force people to eat their food in the dream.

17. **Destiny Manipulators:** They try to thwart God's purpose for promising individuals.

18. **Satanic sexual: partners**

19. **Demon idols**

20. **Spirit Impersonating The Dead:** An old man died at age 91 and was buried. After his demise, the

sound of the walking stick was still being heard for so many days. His son ran to me saying, "Daddy still moves about every night". I sat him down and educated him that it was an impersonating demon that moved about and not the departed soul. I told him that the situation should be arrested or else death would soon catch up with someone else in the family. Prayer was offered and the house and the premises were anointed. Then, the sound ceased.

21.   **Stubborn pursuers**. There are evil arresters.

22.   **Promotion "Shallowers"**

23.   **Desert spirits.**

24.   **Soul fragmentation:** these are spirits that fragment lives and people destiny.

THE LOCATION OF EVIL ARRESTERS

These spirits could be located in the following places.

1.   **Human world**
2.   **Animal world**
3.   **Vegetable world: evil forests and
          bewitched trees**
4.   **Mineral world: underneath the ground**
5.   **Water**
6.   **Storm, wind and forces of nature**

7.   In the heavenlies.

STRATEGIES TO DEAL WITH EVIL ARRESTERS:

There are many strategies. Let us see the prayer strategies of some men who refused to be arrested.

DAVID

The Psalmist employed a holy cry and got results.

Psalm 56:9: When I cry unto thee, then shall mine enemies turn back: this I know; for God is for me.

JACOB

Jacob was the first person to fight his battle through holy cry. What was the prayer point of Jacob? The prayer point is -I will not let you go except you bless me. He prayed that single prayer throughout the night

MOSES

Moses also uttered holy cry into the Lord in Exodus 17.

people surrounded him and they wanted to stone him. He cried unto the Lord

JABEZ

Jabez uttered holy cry unto the Lord. He used four prayer points.

1 Chronicle 4:9-10: And Jabez was more honourable than his brethren: and his mother called his name

Jabez, saying, Because I bare him with sorrow, And Jabez called on the God of Israel, saying, Oh that thou wouldest bless me indeed, and enlarge my coast, and that thine hand might be with me, and that thou wouldest keep me from evil, that it may not grieve me! And God granted him that which he requested.

God answered his prayer and a child of sorrow became a child of blessing.

PETER
Peter the disciple of Christ used one brief prayer point, which goes thus: "Lord save me". This is holy cry arrested the attention of the Lord.

THE SYROPHENICIAN WOMAN
This woman also uttered holy cry unto the Lord. She cried and said, "Have mercy on me oh Lord, thou son of David for my daughter is vexed with an evil spirit".

BLIND BARTIMEUS
The blind man cried "Jesus son of David have mercy on me". This prayer point was short but it received God attention.

SHORT BUT POWERFUL PRAYERS
There are certain things we can gather from these men and women who made use of holy cry as a mean of obtaining their blessings.

The people cried unto the Lord out of desperation. They uttered a holy but desperate cry. The prayers were short and direct but the prayers elicited God's response.

How then can we adopt their form of prayer for our situation?

1. We must pray that angels of our blessings must locate us just as an angel of blessing located Jacob.

2. We need to pray that the angel of our blessing will not go until he blesses us

3. We need to pray the kind of prayer that will provoke angelic assistance.

4. We need to pray after the order of Jabez that the Lord would give us a name that will attract blessing.

5. We can also pray: Let every satanic hindrance targeted against my angel of blessing be devoured with fire.

6. We need to pray that the fountain of infirmity should dry up.

7. We need to ask God to aid us with His mercy.

8. We need to pray that God should keep us from sinking in this life.

PRAYER POINTS

1. Every evil arrester in the heavenlies receive blindness in the name of Jesus.

2. Every power arresting my progress fall down and die in the name of Jesus.

3. I reject every demonic distortion of my destiny in the name of Jesus.

4 Every power contributing stubbornness to my problem fall down and die in the name of Jesus

5. Every power re-arranging my problem fall down and die in the name of Jesus.

6 My angel of blessing must locate me in the name of Jesus.

7. Oh' Lord, deliver me form evil stone thrown at me by unfriendly friend in the name of Jesus.

8. You poison of sickness come out with all your roots in the name of Jesus.

9. Every stubborn pursuer of my health fall down and die in the name of Jesus.

10. My head will not be anchored to any evil thing in the name of Jesus,

Other Publications By Dr. D. K. Olukoya

1. Be Prepared
2. Breakthrough Prayers For Business Professionals
3. Brokenness
4. Born Great, But Tied Down
5. Can God Trust You?
6. Criminals In The House Of God
7. Contending For The Kingdom
8. Dealing With Satanic Exchange
9. Dealing With Local Satanic Technology
10. Dealing With Witchcraft Barbers
11. Dealing With Hidden Curses
12. Dealing With The Evil Powers Of Your Father's House
13. Dealing With Unprofitable Roots
14. Dealing With Tropical Demons
15. Deliverance: God's Medicine Bottle
16. Deliverance From The Limiting Powers
17. Deliverance By Fire
18. Deliverance From Spirit Husband And Spirit Wife
19. Deliverance Of The Conscience
20. Deliverance Of The Head
21. Destiny Clinic
22. Drawers of Power From The Heavenlies
23. Dominion Prosperity
24. Evil Appetite
25. Facing Both Ways
26. Fasting And Prayer
27. Failure In The School Of Prayer
28. For We Wrestle...
29. Holy Cry
30. Holy Fever